Professor Kant's Incredible Day

Professor Kant's Incredible Day

Narrated by
Jean Paul Mongin

Illustrated by
Laurent Moreau

Translated by
Anna Street

Plato & Co.
diaphanes

Königsberg, at the end of the eighteenth century, was a small, peaceful town in East Prussia. Overshadowed by the towers of its famous castle, home to a great many owls and a few prisoners languishing away deep in their dungeons, the ancient city built by the Teutonic Knights had already seen its best days.

We wouldn't even be mentioning the nostalgia of these twilight years, which gripped a lonely stroller on his way home as he turns his back on the vast and dreary plains of Poland, if it weren't for the fact that the stroller was none other than Professor Immanuel Kant.

One day as he was lamenting his lack of a partner to play chess, God decided, so they say, to create Immanuel Kant.

But to be quite frank, Kant wasn't really a very playful person. So he became a philosophy professor in Königsberg.
Martin Heidegger, one of his younger colleagues, who was also quite attached to the plains of Poland, summed up Kant's life by saying, "Kant was born, he worked, and he died."
In Königsberg, we could add.

At the break of dawn one crystal-clear summer morning, Professor Kant's valet Lampe barged into the Professor's bedroom to find him snuggled up in his sheet, apparently lost in a deep, dreamless sleep.

"Time to get up!" Lampe grumbled at his master. As a former Prussian soldier, Lampe had pretty rustic manners. Nonetheless, he awoke the Professor every day at five to five with unfailing punctuality, and that was what really mattered. Without saying a word, Immanuel Kant would get up, allow himself to be shaved and his wig to be powdered. Under his trousers a little system of suspenders made from catgut, threaded through a spring-loaded cylinder, kept his stockings up without cutting off his circulation. Then Kant wound his watch and entered his study in the most dignified of manners to busy himself with his correspondence while smoking his pipe.

Sitting next to the stove, facing the window with a view of the old castle towers, Professor Kant first of all set about responding to whatever foolishness was in fashion. It must be said that lately, reading the newspapers, an activity problems of constipation imposed on him rather often, provided him with more than one irritating topic. But all the same a new low had been reached! In fact, it just so happened that some hare-brained Swede was pretending to be able to predict the future and to communicate with the dead…

The self-proclaimed scholar, Swedenborg, claimed to whoever wanted to listen that he spoke with ghosts. As an example, he cited the widow of a Dutch ambassador who had supposedly, thanks to his services, found the long-lost receipt of a bill for which a dishonest jeweler had been clamoring to receive payment. As it turned out, her late husband had well and truly paid the bill in full seven months before going off to perish who knows where.

"I'll show you and your Dutch ghost flying around with its trinkets—I'll teach it to march in line, I will..." Kant murmured.

“All these efforts to raise humankind up to science, to reject prejudices and superstitions, to spread the light of reason, so much rigor and sacrifice… and then still to read such quackery!” our hero thought.

“As if a specter could have an effect on things! As if the world was nothing more than the delirium of a ghost!”

Professor Kant, with one sweep of his quill, settled his score with the Swede Swedenborg and his visions.

"The uselessness of these kinds of phenomena," he wrote, "the huge amount of difficulties attached to them, the deceit often uncovered as their origin, the gullibility of those who promote them, all of this results in that, in general, I do not bother, nor deem suitable, to feel afraid in a cemetery. The only prophets I know are those who make the future," Kant concluded not without spite.

History remembers Immanuel Kant as a rather sad figure. The dark walls of his house, never brightened by a single young lady coming to visit him, seemed to accommodate nothing but the solitude of his severe meditations.

However, for the Professor, it was through work that life could best be appreciated. Upon brilliantly restoring the empire of reason, such as this morning, Kant couldn't prevent himself from feeling a burst of excitement, giving way to sweet ecstasy.

After making sure that no one would bother him, he had a quick twirl around his astrolabe. In fact, nothing delighted Professor Kant as much as the regularity of this astrolabe which, when its springs and needles were triggered, could shift the tiny planets in order to calculate the predicted position of a celestial body.

“This is what science is!” Kant reflected. “Each day we see the Sun rise and set, as if it were revolving around the Earth. And yet Anatole Copernicus demonstrated that it is truly the Earth which revolves around the Sun!

He didn’t let himself be deceived by common experience, passively observing the changing sky... On the contrary, he assembled and calculated the movements of the stars. By his experiments, he subjected the cosmos to questioning, as a judge compels witnesses to testify.

Copernicus dictated the rules of his own mind to nature, in order to study nature! He formed the object of his knowledge!

It is the Sun, and not the Earth, which is at the center of the universe. It is my mind, and not an object, which is at the center of knowledge... What a revolution!”

This brief moment of gaiety was brought to a brisk end when Professor Kant noticed, in mid-leap, something he hadn't seen earlier: a letter with delicate handwriting lying on his desk. Sensing a serious annoyance to his day, Kant strolled forward, and then became deeply lost in thought.

What letter-opener should be used to open a flowered—
and slightly perfumed—envelope? Most certainly,
his own mind would not have been able to construct such
an incongruous object: this was what was so troubling!

Kant pushed from his thoughts the far-away image of blond curls encircling a fresh face, brimming with excitement, of the Countess Keyserling, in whose home he had once been a private tutor. One night many years ago, the Countess had displayed a curiosity for philosophical pursuits that went beyond the young tutor's expectations, since he had been employed in order to provide "instruction in the art of conversation," as he put it.

Upon examining himself honestly, he wondered whether anyone would be able to recognize, and perhaps still love, the real Immanuel Kant behind this individual who seemed to him to be of rather small stature, with a practically concave chest and a domed forehead protruding over dark eyes. “One could say that this is the case for all the things I encounter…” mused Kant. “I do not see myself as others see me because a mirror always reflects back an opposite image. I do not see the world exactly as others see it, either. And no one can see the world as it is in itself!”

Awakening from these reflections and suddenly remembering the lecture he had to give, the Professor stuffed the letter, still sealed, in his pocket, grabbed his three-cornered hat and his rapier, and took off for the University of Königsberg. On his way, he passed only once over each of the seven bridges of the city, following an itinerary of which no one since has ever been able to discover the secret.

At the end of his path, Kant caught sight of his friend Jean-Jacques Rousseau doing somersaults in a park. "Good day to you, Jean-Jacques, the Newton of morals!" he called out.

Professor Kant used to despise ignorant people, placing knowledge above all else, even if he never refused a game of pool or a glass of wine. Jean-Jacques had shown him that within the diversity of races and cultures resides the unity of human nature, and had taught him to respect it.

Currently, Jean-Jacques no longer spoke of philosophy, and spent the better part of his time cultivating his herbarium. His research of botanical curiosities rarely led him all the way to Königsberg. Kant was dying to show him the letter he had received, but decided against it: Jean-Jacques probably understood nothing about matters of love.

At the university, Kant took his place in front of his desk as though facing an anvil and delivered his lecture as though he were a blacksmith hammering iron.

"Human knowledge," he hammered out to his students squeezed about him and spilling out into the hallway, "is of two sorts: on one side, you have what can be learned by experience, such as the peculiar taste of eel soup; on the other side, you have what is universal and necessary, what can be learned by the use of reason, as in mathematics or philosophy. In mathematics, one starts from indisputable definitions, for example, equations.

In philosophy, to the contrary, I try to produce these definitions. This is why philosophers ask so many questions... What can I know? What should I do? What may I hope? What's for dinner?

In the end, what philosophy tries to define is how I must use my thinking powers, to serve what end. Philosophy is the science of final purposes, of the ultimate aim of human reason. In other words, philosophy is the idea of perfect wisdom. It's very concrete, as you can see: one does not learn philosophy. One learns to philosophize."

"Oh! Reason, our marvelous and cruel mistress... On all of us, she weighs down with questions that are impossible to brush aside, such as knowing if God exists, if our soul is immortal, if we are free... And we find ourselves with the other philosophers in the supernatural arena where gladiatorial strength is matched in ceremonial combats, but with never a champion having been able to make himself conqueror of even the slightest ground. I can prove that God exists; I can prove that He does not exist. Admit that it's really rather confusing!

Before approaching such a problem, we must therefore submit reason to a critique. Science must be called to appear in court, in order to reveal its legitimate claims and its limitations. Then we discover that science cannot provide answers to all questions. To know something, I must be able to situate it in space and in time, which are the conditions, or the framework that my mind gives to all experience. And it is impossible to examine God within space and time! You understand why one must not fall asleep on one's beliefs or else you don't understand anything and you are telling yourselves that I am really the great Chinaman of Königsberg..."

The students laughed, but Professor Kant remained completely serious.

"I am not speaking of faith here, I am speaking of knowledge. Take liberty, for example, a free act," he continued. "Have you ever done anything completely freely, absolutely unselfishly? It could be doubted. We will never know. A free act cannot be explained, or else it is no longer free. Because we cannot conceive of something happening, just like that, out of nowhere. There is no beginning in nature, only a series of causes and effects.

Take the example of a liar. If we wanted to explain his deed, we could say that he was encouraged to lie because he got in with a bad crowd, or that he was destined from his earliest days to commit evil, that he is simply following his destiny… Where is the liberty in that?"

Speaking of that particular day, several students would testify that Professor Kant ascended to the sky armed with his metaphysical machine gun, having massacred the supernatural garrison, drowned God in its blood, disemboweled liberty, and left the immortal soul for dead.

Then, noticing the stupor on the faces of his audience following the terrifying slaughter he had just executed in the realm of knowledge, Professor Kant decided to become indulgent, to bring God, liberty and the immortal soul back to life in the moral realm with a wag of his magic wand.

"Rest assured," he said with a little smile. "It is not because we cannot prove liberty, the existence of God, and the immortality of the soul that we cannot think them. These questions may, while having no answer of a scientific nature, be able to be resolved from a moral point of view.

If we accuse the liar I evoked earlier of having lied, it can only be because we consider him responsible for his crime! And thus free! Out with fatalism, down with extenuating circumstances, end of story! String him up, the liar! How's that for concrete?!

In practice, we must assume that we are responsible for our actions, that our souls will live on, and that God will reward men of good will in due time... for if not, would it not be better to be wicked and happy rather than upright and unhappy?"

Professor Kant left the University of Königsberg crushed by the weight of his own genius. Sometimes he wearied of himself and the world in this way. But today, a dash of brave enthusiasm broke through his customary melancholy. Kant knew very well that philosophy would not make him happy, as happiness does not come along to ratify knowledge, but, on the other hand, he did have that sweet letter in his pocket...

When he found himself facing the Königsberg harbor, Kant stepped into a tavern he liked to frequent, ordered a cup of coffee, and opened the letter without any further ado.

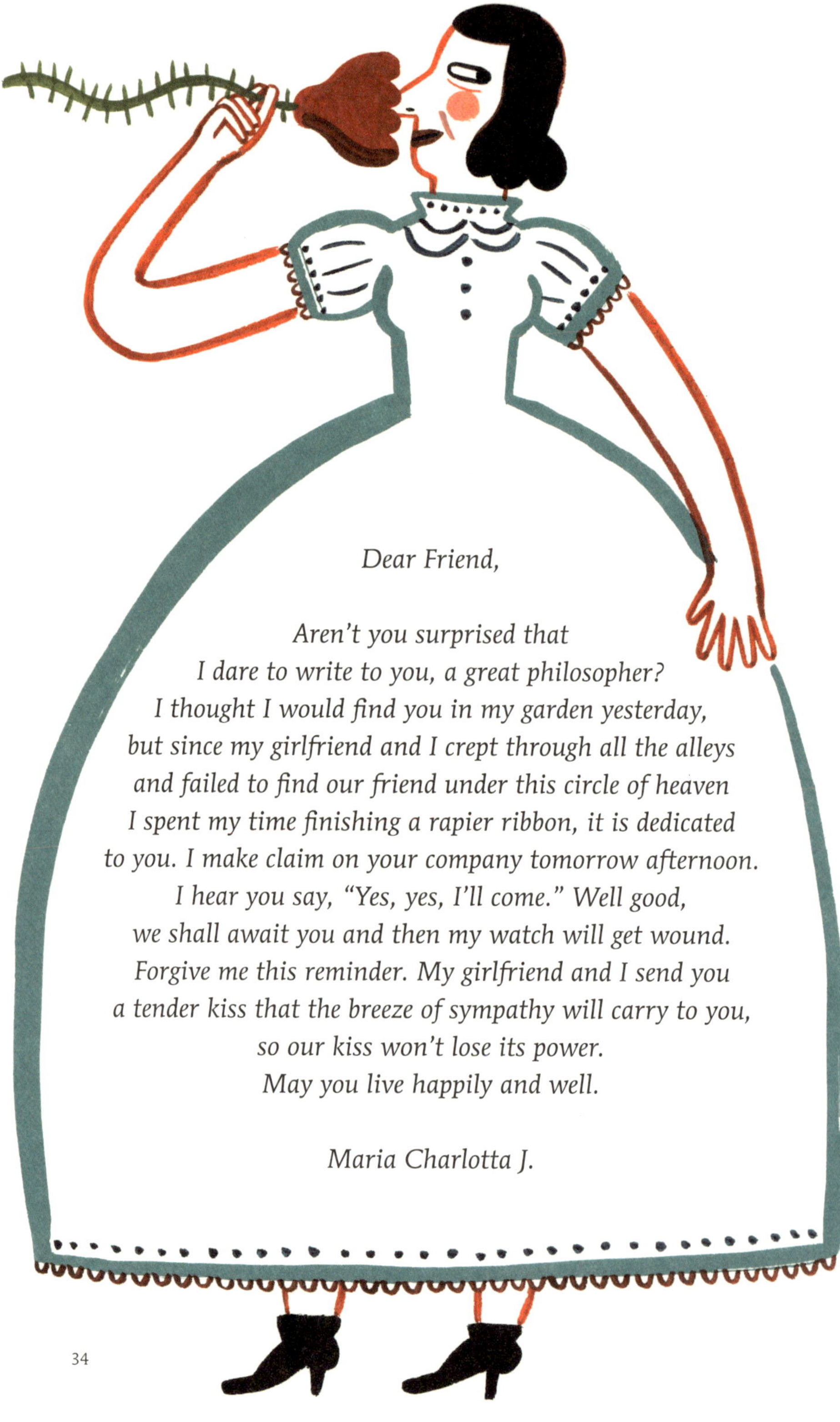

Dear Friend,

Aren't you surprised that
I dare to write to you, a great philosopher?
I thought I would find you in my garden yesterday,
but since my girlfriend and I crept through all the alleys
and failed to find our friend under this circle of heaven
I spent my time finishing a rapier ribbon, it is dedicated
to you. I make claim on your company tomorrow afternoon.
I hear you say, "Yes, yes, I'll come." Well good,
we shall await you and then my watch will get wound.
Forgive me this reminder. My girlfriend and I send you
a tender kiss that the breeze of sympathy will carry to you,
so our kiss won't lose its power.
May you live happily and well.

Maria Charlotta J.

Maria Charlotta was much younger than Professor Kant. She came and went with extraordinary lightness, as inspired by her flirtatiousness and the military operations of Russian or Prussian officers. She wasn't very smart, but could tell when someone else was. She was the opposite of the kind of woman that Kant couldn't stand, the Amazonian sort who argued mechanics or meddled with ancient Greek! As for those women, all they lacked was a beard to better express the depths of their minds!

In Professor Kant's opinion, the rapier ribbon enclosed in the letter was a ravishing delicacy, and the allusion to the wound watch, well, a bit mischievous.

Tantalized, the great Chinaman of Königsberg savored the summer breeze coming through the harbor as he contemplated the dance of the ships coming from fantastical lands, loaded with the spices or coffee which he thoroughly enjoyed. In addition to mathematics and pyrotechnics, Kant had spent part of his career teaching geography in profuse detail.

Yet he had traveled so little that he had never seen a desert or even the crest of a mountain. However, two imaginary Scottish ancestors, innumerable social chats, the narratives of explorations borrowed from the royal library, and lastly, the crew at the harbor gave him the opportunity to think deeply on the species inhabiting the earth and national characteristics...

"The fish named Beluga," proclaimed Kant, "for example, common in Russia during the floods of the river Volga, swallow big rocks in order to weigh themselves down and stay at the bottom of the water. Meanwhile, drunkenness is more prevalent in Siberia than anywhere else...
The Spaniard is serious, discreet and very proud. If you walk in front of him while he's busy with his plow, he will pace up and down his field wearing his long coat, brandishing his sword."

"The French are, above all, witty.
The English, prudent and stubborn, easily regarded as eccentric, despise anything unfamiliar to them.
The Germans are honest and methodical in everything, even in love.

As for the inhabitants of other planets, they are as ethereal as their star is distant from the sun ... The inhabitants of Venus or of Mercury are thus extremely heavy.
The first Eskimo of Greenland would be like Newton next to them! On the other hand, the inhabitants of Jupiter have marvelously light-weight bodies."

If Immanuel Kant came to the harbor for his cup of coffee, it is because this beverage, which he had a difficult time digesting, was forbidden at home. In addition, he felt close to the sailor preparing for his voyage in search of the island of pure intelligence, the country of truth.

All around him stretched vast and stormy oceans, like the appearances of this world, offering only thick fog, fragile ice floes, and illusions of new lands. These waves with their vain hopes appealed to the sailor-philosopher who dreamed of discoveries and of adventures which he could not bring himself to renounce, though they remain unachieved.

Would it not be better to stay on firm ground, to content oneself with that and to defend it against hostile claims, while passing to pay a visit to Maria Charlotta in the afternoon?

ES IST ZEIT!

Lampe, the valet, entered the living room at one o'clock sharp to announce to his master, "It is time!" Professor Kant had made it home just in time to welcome his guests. He never ate his only meal of the day alone because it ruined his appetite. His daydreaming caused him bad digestion, the cause of all mental illnesses. The number of guests varied between that of the Graces, meaning three, and that of the Muses, nine, so that the conversation never flagged nor wandered off. In fact, Kant usually met up with the same visitors from one day to the next.

Thus there was an English merchant who came regularly to our philosopher's home. He had met Kant in a tavern, where the latter had been affirming his support for American independence. The merchant, as a British subject, had been offended and had challenged him to a duel.

Kant had pretended to draw his rapier then changed his mind because he was very poor at fencing. Forcing himself to justify his position by basing it on his esteem for England, he had kept talking about the people's liberty. He had carried on for so long and so well that he and Joseph Green had made up and become friends.

On that day, a young French philosopher, who had traveled from Paris to attend Professor Kant's class and to discuss moral doctrine, was also present.

Professor Kant took it upon himself to jump-start the conversation by telling a few jokes he knew well. So he told the story of an heir who was unable to throw a proper funeral for his benefactor since the more money he gave to the mourners, the more joyful they became.

His joke not being quite as successful as he had hoped, Kant described a terrible storm out at sea, in which a rich merchant's small boat was caught.
"In order to save the vessel, the merchant was forced to throw his entire fortune overboard! And do you know what happened? It was not the merchant's hair that turned grey... but his wig!!!"

For Professor Kant, laughter eased digestion, which led him to share with Mr. Green and the French philosopher some reflections about practical hygiene. Kant could talk forever about the ill effects of beer or of electricity, and he recommended washing one's feet with ice water in order to avoid weakness of the arteries furthest from the heart. He described dizzy spells caused by thinking while walking, something he couldn't manage to prevent himself from doing. Lastly, his fool-proof remedy for insomnia was to think of Cicero, the Roman orator.

From Kant's point of view, each person should determine what best preserves one's health according to one's constitution, for example quick-tempered or fiery. Himself melancholic, the philosopher soothed his pathological restlessness with a strict diet. But melancholic persons, having a high opinion of human nature, more easily obeyed their conscience.

“Professor,” interrupted the French philosopher, “is one more or less moral by constitution?”

“I’m only talking about predispositions,” Immanuel Kant responded in a very serious voice. “So long as you possess reason, you are always absolutely free to act morally, no matter your constitution or the circumstances.”

“Nevertheless, there are always circumstances which affect the way in which a crime is perceived. The liar in your lecture from this morning, whom you sent to the gallows, perhaps lied in order to protect someone. Lying is sometimes more moral than telling the truth...”

“It’s even possible to make one’s profession out of it,” joked the merchant Mr. Green.

“I’m not following you, gentlemen,” replied Kant. “A lie is a contradiction between speech and thought; it destroys the very essence of speech, which is trust. Any discourse promises truth, even that of a liar. That is why lying is the most contradictory of deeds, and thus the most immoral.”

“Have you never lied, Kant?” asked Mr. Green, who did not easily let himself be distracted when being served Göttingen sausages.

"Of course I have, and I feel ashamed every time I think of it."

"But suppose that a friend is hiding in your home, pursued by an assassin," asked the French philosopher. "If the assassin questions you about your friend's hiding place, you would lie to him, wouldn't you?"

"I would rather refuse to answer him, I imagine."

"But suppose that you are forced to answer?"

"If I must answer him," said Professor Kant, "I would tell him the truth. Telling the truth remains a duty, even if it results in serious disadvantages."

"He will kill your friend! That would indeed be a serious disadvantage!" Mr. Green burst out beaming.

"How do you know that? Maybe the neighbors will arrive in time to prevent him from doing it. Maybe my friend will have escaped, and the assassin would run into him right in the street had I told him that he wasn't at my house. But no matter! Honesty is a duty! If we tolerate the least exception, then there can be no moral doctrine."

"My dear Kant, you are a terrorist," Mr. Green said playfully.

"Professor, I'd rather have you as an idol than as a friend!" said the French philosopher.

"Oh, my friend, there is no friend," smiled Kant, quoting Aristotle.

"Do you want to know what is truly moral? That which can be considered as absolutely good?" Immanuel Kant started up again.

"Intelligence," proposed the French philosopher. "Intelligence is what makes science progress!"

"Health," replied the practical Mr. Green.

"Oh, come on! Intelligence, health? But if we endowed a bandit with intelligence, health or courage, he would only be more dangerous… he would become… a kind of evil genius! No, I'm telling you, the only thing absolutely good is the will to do the good."

"Yet it remains to be known what is the good!" remarked Mr. Green.

"There is no need for any science to be honest and good," replied Kant. "One needs merely to act as everyone should act. I speak the truth because I want all men everywhere to always speak the truth. I treat humanity, whether myself or another, always as an end in itself, and never simply as a means."

"What a beautiful moral law," acknowledged the two guests.

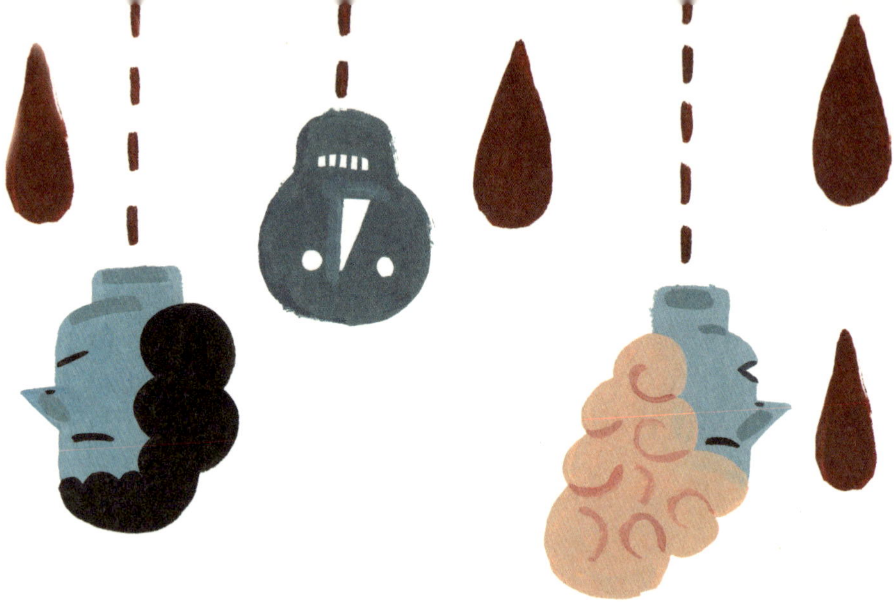

Then the news from Paris was brought up. The young French philosopher told how the general assembly, summoned by King Louis XVI in order to pay for his wife's earrings, had degenerated into absolute confusion. The deputies of the third estate, dragging along with them several nobles and clergymen, had interrupted a game of royal tennis. In reaction, heads began to be cut off frenetically, something which confirmed all the same a rather sharp reorientation from the light-hearted and witty disposition which Professor Kant attributed to the French.

The said professor's opinions were divided: on the one hand, all of this forecast wide-spread anarchy, something which Kant loathed above all. Interrupt a game of royal tennis! Who could imagine a more appalling crime?

On the other hand, even if this revolution had begun in the greatest disorder and illegality, the new order which was beginning to take shape received his undivided sympathy. The perspective of equilibrium and a clear distinction between the legislative power, which makes the laws, the executive power, which governs according to these laws, and the judicial power, which guarantees that these laws be respected, appeared to him to be progress. Whether or not Louis XVI stayed on the throne, it was the end of tyranny. Universal peace would eventually install itself among all peoples, perhaps even among philosophers. The unsocial sociability of man, which propels him, for love of honor, appetite for power or greed, to make his place amongst his fellow creatures, would be reconciled in the triumph of law...

The valet, Lampe, on whom not a single word of the conversation had been lost, dashed to his room to get his pistols, sharpen his old spade and hide his savings.

It is said that on the day in question, Immanuel Kant stayed at home, preoccupied by the announcement of the French Revolution. But according to other accounts, Kant, summoned by the sweet Maria Charlotta, slipped out discreetly through the backyard. Sporting a shirt of crisp lace and a new rapier ribbon, the Professor would have actually passed a very romantic afternoon.

"O woman, you have so often eluded me!" he would have whispered to Maria Charlotta. "You drive me towards ideal excitements and progressively from purely animal desire to love! With love, the feeling of all that is pleasant becomes a liking for your beauty. My imagination plays unhampered with my understanding, and looking at you, I feel alive! Oh, Maria Charlotta, you are more beautiful than the most beautiful of flowers! You are as beautiful as... my astrolabe!"

No one knows if this fiery declaration was met with success.

What we do know, however, is that Professor Kant did not go on his digestive walk.
For this stroll, usually so regular, had virtually become Königsberg's time reference. For the longest time, the people of Königsberg set their clocks by the philosopher's after-lunch promenade.

Consequently, without this walk, Königsberg, and indeed, the entire universe, was plunged into chaos. The pastor forgot the church service. The pharmacist, of alchemist tendencies, left his decoction on the stove, which exploded, giving out toxic fumes. The hermit who lived at the edge of the Königsberg woods started screaming his head off. A great number of cats died.

In Sweden, the seer Swedenborg was smitten with terrible visions, and for all these reasons, or for none of them, clouds gathered over the little Prussian town, forecasting a terrifying tempest of blood and toads raining down.

Professor Kant, quite occupied as he was with meditating on the beautiful and the pleasant, made a passing remark which would provide a new foundation for metaphysics: "Look, a storm is coming."

Kant had barely arrived in his cellar when the thunder's roar made the ground of Königsberg tremble, causing a sack of flour to spill over right at our philosopher's feet. All powdered white, he lit a candle and discovered that the sack had harbored a nest. A swallow nestled within, surrounded by lifeless fledglings.

The weather had been chilly that year, and insects rare. The bird, unable to feed all her babies, had probably had to sacrifice some in order to save the others. Kant cupped the swallow in his hands, looked into its eyes and tried to read its mind. He had the feeling he was peering into the sky.

Upstairs, the storm was upsetting the piles of books and sending the little balls of the astrolabe into a whirl. Kant reached his study and opened the window. He noticed that the church tower had been struck by lightning and was ablaze. A new lightning bolt, accompanied by a deafening roar, sent a shiver down his spine. Professor Kant was terrified and fascinated at the same time. How small everything seemed in comparison to this storm!

Mindless of the gusts of rain lashing his face, Kant contemplated this sublime, unleashed nature in the twilight, as though it were an image of his own mind.

Night fell on Königsberg. The storm abated. The rain stopped and the clouds dispersed. The inhabitants, gathered in the square before the burning church, were the very picture of troubled humanity. Immanuel Kant winked at the portrait of his friend Jean-Jacques Rousseau, hanging over his writing case. He had never felt such pure joy.

“Two things,” he said aloud, “fill my mind with ever-increasing wonder and awe: the starry heavens above me and the moral law within me.”

Professor Kant breathed in the night air for a few moments. Then he mopped his brow and with a smile on his lips, wound his watch.

French edition
Jean Paul Mongin & Laurent Moreau:
La Folle Journée du Professeur Kant
Design: Yohanna Nguyen

First edition
ISBN 978-3-03734-595-5

www.platoandco.net
www.diaphanes.com

Layout: 2edit, Zurich
Printed and bound in Germany